Feast of the Marys

Steve Dixon

© Copyright 2020 Steve Dixon

All rights reserved.
No part of this publication may be reproduced, stored in a retrieval system, or transmitted, in any form or by any means, electronic, mechanical, photocopying, recording or otherwise, without the prior written permission of the publisher.

British Library Cataloguing in Publication Data.
A catalogue record for this book is available from the British Library

978 0 86071 839 0

A Commissioned Publication Printed by
info@moorleys.co.uk • www.moorleys.co.uk

The Scripture quotations contained herein are from the New Revised Standard Version Bible, copyright © 1989 by the Division of Christian Education of the National Council of the Churches of Christ in the U. S. A. and are used by permission. All rights reserved.

for Joan

Contents

Introduction   1

Lady of Our Joys
I	A Pregnancy is Announced	4
II	Sisterhood	5
III	A New Life	6
IV	Visitors	7
V	Rejoicing	8
VI	Parents' Evening	9
VII	Local Hero	10

Lady of Our Sorrows
I	Our Lady of Sorrows	12
II	Our Lady, Star of the Sea	13
III	Our Lady of Grace	14
IV	Our Lady of Good Counsel	15
V	Our Lady of Mercy	16
VI	Our Lady of Miracles	18
VII	Our Lady of Compassion	19

Lady of Our Lives
I	Our Lady of the Waters	22
II	Our Lady of the Rocks	23
III	Our Lady of the Sun	24
IV	Our Lady of Humility	25
V	Our Lady of the Pines	26
VI	Our Lady of the Wayside	27
VII	Our Lady of the Snows	29

Acknowledgements   30

Introduction

During the last few years I have spent periods of time in the Canaries and Italy – both places where there are many churches dedicated to Mary, often with specific links to places or conditions of life, such as 'Our Lady of the Pines' or 'Our Lady of the Snows'. This has led me to an interest in the way that Mary, as a mother, can stand as a bridge between the Christian story of faith and our everyday stories of joy and sorrow; and as a young woman of humble origin, yet 'highly favoured' by God, can intimate God's presence in the simple activities of daily life. The poems in this collection are an attempt to explore links between Mary's story and ours.

In the first sequence, *Lady of Our Joys*, the voice in the poems could be Mary's, or it could be yours, or that of anyone who has nurtured a growing life. The last stanza of each poem in the second sequence, *Lady of Our Sorrows,* invokes Mary under one of her traditional titles. The voice of these poems is definitely not that of Mary but is a contemporary expression of the sorrows that seem to resonate with Mary's story. Again, it could be your voice, it could be mine or that of anyone who loves. The final sequence, *Lady of Our Lives,* uses associations of Mary with everyday locations, scenes, seasonal events and activities, derived from church dedications, to suggest a thread of blessing weaving through the ordinary things of life. 'Feast of the Marys'*,* from which this collection takes its title, was an event I saw advertised on the noticeboard of a Canarian church.

Steve Dixon
August 2020

Lady of Our Joys

I A Pregnancy is Announced
you will conceive in your womb. (Luke 1. 31)

Blue will be my colour –
the brilliant blue of the holy sky
the deepest blue of the sea.
I am floating and flying
upheld by the fingers of miracle
rolling gently between heaven and earth.
My ears ring with the song of angels
my body is alive with the touch of God
creation is recreated within me
and I shall see that all is good.

II   Sisterhood

as soon as I heard the sound of your greeting, the child in my womb leapt for joy. (Luke 1. 44)

Everywhere I look
I see pregnant women.
Who would have thought
there was so much hope in the world!
Everywhere cousins, sisters –
I have a family in every land.
We exchange secret looks
whisper secret words.
Inside, our children stir.
We smile. We know
we are freighted with the power
that will save us.

III   A New Life

the time came for her to deliver her child. (Luke 2. 6)

There is a universe
of possibility in
my baby's face

sleeping, closed
in on itself – recovering
from the journey

awake, eyes
gazing relentlessly
focussing the blur

learning me
teaching me
generous gift.

IV   Visitors

On entering the house, they saw the child with Mary his mother. (Matthew 2. 11)

We hold court
baby and I
receive embassies
and regal visits
from the farthest
reaches of our world.
For this time
we are the centre
of all worlds.
The gifts pile up
and formal good
wishes, blessings.
All seem strange
ill-judged
clumsily put.
The only needful gift is
in my arms
wordless.
Breath
the only cogent blessing.

V   Rejoicing

they brought him up to Jerusalem to present him to the Lord. (Luke 2. 22)

I have rejoiced together
with my husband
my family and his
our neighbours and friends.
I have stopped people
I hardly know
to give them my news.
I have yearned to share with
strangers – though modesty forbade.

But today my yearning
has found its home.
I have shared my joy
with the One who knows.
We have held each other
close, crooned
warmed each other's hearts.
Now my rejoicing
is complete.

VI   Parents' Evening

all who heard him were amazed at his understanding.
(Luke 2. 47)

Never more other than now.
Shoulder-high, yet meeting
the teachers as equals –
not so much in knowledge
as wisdom and maturity.
Courteous. Polite questioning.
Speaking up in the cause
of truth, not vanity.

They are a community of otherness
faces lit by a shared passion
teachers and pupil
excited explorers together.
I hang back a moment
reluctant to disturb
warmed by their radiance
excluded but elated.

The bond of flesh is my only
link to this other life
a world that is beyond me.
My scholar conducts
me round the classroom.
When we set out for home
lightly holding hands
I am unclear who is the child.

VII Local Hero

Where did this man get this wisdom and these deeds of power? Is not this the carpenter's son? Is not his mother called Mary? (Matthew 13. 54-55)

Lately your name
is on everyone's tongue.
I hear it and turn
to see strangers talking.

'You must be so proud,'
friends say. What have I
to be proud of who
was only your vessel?

Your life is making
a difference for good
therefore, so has mine
that carried you.

Not proud, then, but glad
you're at work in the world –
glad I was the ark
that bore you to land.

Lady of Our Sorrows

I   Our Lady of Sorrows

a sword will pierce your own soul. (Luke 2. 35)

Who needs a prophet? Just look out
of the window, or into the screen.
Everything precious, worthy, noble
writhes like a rag in a storm.

To love is to put yourself into the power
of fear and those who would crush,
tear, shred, erase or deface
the fragile and defenceless.

O God, where's the sense! What hunger feeds
on the slender meat of the weak?
What weakness draws strength from smashing
the tiny gains of the poor?

And into this are children born
to this my child is given.
Their names shall be called in desperation –
'Come home safe! Come home!'

Our Lady of Sorrows – of our sorrows –
soften the heart of evil.
Soak it in the tears of love.
Give courage in dangerous times.

II Our Lady, Star of the Sea

Get up, take the child and his mother, and flee.
(Matthew 2. 13)

There is nowhere to run –
they hate us everywhere.
Nowhere to hide –
they smell us out.
The only choice
a slit throat here
or there a spit in the eye.
Nowhere to run
but still we flee.
Home? We have no home
until the ones
who want us dead
have died.

Star of the Sea
scintilla of hope
night flight's light
anchored point in
wrecking storm
glimmer as
we struggle on.

III   Our Lady of Grace

the boy Jesus stayed behind in Jerusalem, but his parents did not know it. (Luke 2. 43)

You are no longer part of me.
The moment the cord was cut
your blood was your own.

The cord was cut, and yet I feel,
like a ghost of amputation,
its tugging still.

You stand at a distance, facing me
a challenge in your eyes,
beloved stranger.

Our Lady of Grace
open our hands to your blessing –
holy releasing.

IV   Our Lady of Good Counsel

do not weep for me, but weep for yourselves and for your children. (Luke 23. 28)

Our choices are
what make us and destroy us
and those we love.
Don't mess with death, choose life!

Pushing the swing too high,
hitching round Europe,
joining the army, police,
refusing the draft,

marching with medicines
into the midst of mayhem,
confronting a racist
whose face is bunched like a fist,

when times are hard, declining
the chance of a lifetime
with strings attached,
handing back a backhander,

standing your ground
as the tanks advance,
bearing a child in this world.
Choose life, and pay.

Our Lady of Good Counsel
light in the clouds
whisper your wisdom
on the *via dolorosa*.

V   Our Lady of Mercy

My God, my God, why have you forsaken me?
(Mark 15. 34 quoting Psalm 22. 1)

Looking for her doll in the rubble –
a wall just fell on her.
It groaned and crumpled
and that was her, gone.
When we dug her out
she had the doll in her hand,
both of them flattened.

The needle killed him. Tainted.
Started when he was at school.
Someone gave him a free sample
on his way home.
He looked 50 when he died –
he was only 33.
I found him dead in the toilet.

Drunk driver
ploughed through a bus queue.
On her way to work,
couldn't afford a car,
was saving, taking lessons.
Drunk didn't even have a licence.
'Yes, that's her,' I told them at the morgue.

'I'll swing for you!' That was the phrase.
His wife said he didn't swing.
Hung absolutely still.
The whole house still.
Like opening the door on a frozen world.
There was a letter on the kitchen table –
a fortnight's notice, after 30 years.

Our Lady of Mercy
we huddle beneath your mantle
driven by our loss,
clutch each other fiercely,
silent, trembling
as the arrows of our annihilation
rattle on your cloak like hail.

VI   Our Lady of Miracles

he took [the body] down, wrapped it in a linen cloth.
(Luke 23. 53)

I told him not to go out.
Hear shouting in the street, you lock the door.
Don't twitch the curtain
or you'll be sweeping up broken glass.

I watched from the door – over in seconds.
Three lads kicking a fourth,
my lad shouting –
'Pack it in now – he's had enough.'

Arms wide – open target.
One punch to the chest
and down he went.
Knife glint in the streetlight.

Three lads running, one lad crawling,
mine dead in my arms.
I rocked him, hugged him.
His pierced body oozed blood.

Our Lady of Miracles,
will the blood wash out?
Can the dead return?
Did you ever find peace?

VII   Our Lady of Compassion

Now there was a garden in the place where he was crucified, and in the garden there was a new tomb. (John 19. 41)

He always loved a garden –
'Nearer to God,' he'd say –
away from the crowds,
smell the flowers, chirpy birds,
breeze shaking the leaves.
This is a nice one. Nice view
if you turn your back
on the place where he died.
In other circs
he'd have liked it here.

We'll hold a vigil tonight.
Family and friends,
light candles, lay flowers,
cards – the usual things.
Perhaps it'll help. Expect it will.
We can hold each other, cry a bit.
Then, in time, maybe they'll let us
pay for a bench in his memory.
Nice brass plate, with his details –
Taken too early. Always alive in our hearts.

☆

Our Lady of Compassion,
suffering with us,
hold our hands as we grip yours.
Place a lily on our shrines.

Lady of Our Lives

I   Our Lady of the Waters

Skeins of light swayed as she swayed:
her bucket had scooped light.
It dazzled her eyes,
ran along the curve beneath her chin
rippled under the cottage eaves,
liquid light in an arc as she poured.
Then light became music:
the stream at the bottom of the hill
sounded like rilling light.
And this was spring.

And this is spring:
cracked tarmac and green lances,
drizzle and shop doorways,
crossing the road in a daze,
honking car horns, angry gestures.
Hope of better days;
memory of better days, with no regret.
Above the rip of the living street
hint of a slender, tumbling tune –
rilling of liquid light.

II   Our Lady of the Rocks

Before the light of dawn is fully broken,
the rumble of diesel engines across the deep
gives notice of the fishing fleet's return.
Tired eyes seek the first assurance of safety:
the blessing of her beacon on the headland.
The greater light of the sun, silvering the harvest
heaved onto the quay, takes second place in the heart.

As a weary trudge from the fields marks the end of toil,
as whistles, bells, buzzers or clicking clocks
signal 'tools down' for another day,
as coats are donned, bags or cases gripped,
buses, trains and traffic queues endured,
in dusky minds her light gives strength and hope,
and a rock is added to the cairn of gratitude.

III   Our Lady of the Sun

She sees the couple
hand in hand, barely clothed,
walking the ridge – silhouettes
against a summer sky.

They are leading each other
to the leafy aisle
and sacred arbour
where lovers join.

She gives them time –
enjoys the lick of sweat on her skin,
the delicate touch of an emerald fly,
the choral hum of bees exploring,

then burst of joyful birdsong,
and blossoms in full blow –
their perfume, released,
flooding the breathless air.

They are sleeping now.
Sun through the canopy
scatters petals of light
on their fragrant flesh.

All their lives to come
will rest on these bright days.
She weaves twin crowns of flowers,
to place upon their holy brows.

IV   Our Lady of Humility

She shall not give suck in the shadows
but in a halo of glory
atop the holy hill;
and around her, taking sweet sabbath rest,
the fire crews who cannot forget
the ones they could not save,
the social workers whose bulging files
of heartache always wait,
the nurses made dizzy by the clamour of need,
the carers working against the clock,
the human rights campaigners
whose war will never end,
the medical convoy drivers
dreaming of dangerous roads,
the soup kitchen helpers, night shelter staff,
Street Angels, the homeless who share their bread,
and all whose lives are milk for the world.
Alleluias shall ring around them.

And the chief executives, haggling
for yet more millions in pay
shall do their dirty work
in the grubby back-rooms of shame.

V   Our Lady of the Pines

At the heart of the continent,
a new-grown stand of pines.
Among them, still as a monument,
an old, old man recalls.

Three generations past,
a factory made munitions here:
defeated remnants of its walls
decay among the trunks.
The old man stares,
feels his boyhood fingers
fumbling with freezing steel –
a starved slave among slaves.

A tearful woman brought him
here today, wrapped him warm
against the autumn chill,
eager to receive his testament.
Might she be a granddaughter?
So many weddings and births –
his descendants flicker like stars.
He can no longer name them all.

The land is stripped for death
but the pines have not disarmed.
Their roots probe concrete foundations,
patiently invade – and shatter them.

VI   Our Lady of the Wayside

Her lullabies
are my earliest memories,
those and her laughter,
firm grip, cool hands.

We skipped together
along the pavement.
She lifted me high,
tossed into sunlight.

Her patience made
letters my friends
and words my tools
to grasp and shape the world.

She would stop mid-lesson,
mid-sentence, walk to the window,
gaze at a squirrel or swaying branch.
Her eyes taught mine to see.

In dark bars and cafes,
or private, curtained places
she would cradle my fractured heart.
Her life, too, had known its hurts.

After the cheers and applause,
the handshakes and presentations,
her knowing, smiling eyes
perfected all my triumphs.

She delivered my babies,
admired and blessed them,
encouraged and steadied
my nervous hands.

At the head of every table
for birthdays, weddings, wakes,
her silent presence
held all things in their place.

Easing my brittle bones
between the laundered sheets,
her butterfly kiss and murmured prayer
are my last things.

VII   Our Lady of the Snows

The land was close to dead, we feared.
Drought had lasted through till winter.
Leaves had shrivelled, fallen early.
People stared at bony branches,
bowed their heads and hurried on.
Perhaps they'd never bud again.
The ground was like a sutured skull
no sweet shower could revive.
Sudden storms, repulsed, defeated,
roared away in flood and wreckage.

Then came snow – the silent gift:
a sickbed blanket for the land,
astonishing as answered prayer.
At first no cries or snowballs flew –
we stood on doorsteps, mute, and marvelled.
And then, from nowhere, a woman danced –
danced in her nightshift, white as wings.
Snow fell again and filled her footprints.
Beneath the blanket, moisture seeped,
loosened, and renewed the earth.

Acknowledgements

The author gratefully acknowledges the support, encouragement and wise comments of the Penistone Poets, with whom some of these poems were workshopped.

A selection from 'Feast of the Marys' was read by the author as part of a reflective afternoon entitled 'Mary Today', hosted by William Temple Church, Wythenshawe, in March 2019. Several of the poems have also been used in worship and as reflective material with the Upper Holme Valley Team Ministry.

VII   Our Lady of the Snows

The land was close to dead, we feared.
Drought had lasted through till winter.
Leaves had shrivelled, fallen early.
People stared at bony branches,
bowed their heads and hurried on.
Perhaps they'd never bud again.
The ground was like a sutured skull
no sweet shower could revive.
Sudden storms, repulsed, defeated,
roared away in flood and wreckage.

Then came snow – the silent gift:
a sickbed blanket for the land,
astonishing as answered prayer.
At first no cries or snowballs flew –
we stood on doorsteps, mute, and marvelled.
And then, from nowhere, a woman danced –
danced in her nightshift, white as wings.
Snow fell again and filled her footprints.
Beneath the blanket, moisture seeped,
loosened, and renewed the earth.

Acknowledgements

The author gratefully acknowledges the support, encouragement and wise comments of the Penistone Poets, with whom some of these poems were workshopped.

A selection from 'Feast of the Marys' was read by the author as part of a reflective afternoon entitled 'Mary Today', hosted by William Temple Church, Wythenshawe, in March 2019. Several of the poems have also been used in worship and as reflective material with the Upper Holme Valley Team Ministry.